The Wasp-Mimicking

Longhorn Beetles

A Photographic Journey Through Five *Necydalis* Species

Necydalis gigantea gigantea Kano, 1933. (Jun. 25, 2023, 14:40, Nagano Pref.)

Office Atact

Insect in the Landscape

ISBN: 9798304101271

I extend my heartfelt gratitude to *Necydalis*, which never ceases to fascinate me.

Necydalis niimurai Hayashi, 1949, stat. rev. (Jul. 3, 2016, 12:24, Yamanashi. Pref.)

CONTENTS

Preface

1 Why Mimic Wasps? 3

2 Introduction to Five Species of *Necydalis* Beetles 8

    1) *Necydalis niimurai* 9

    2) *Necydalis solida* 15

    3) *Necydalis harmandi harmandi* 21

    4) *Necydalis odai* 24

    5) *Necydalis gigantea gigantea* 27

3 Videos of Three Species of *Necydalis* Beetles 33

4 Afterword 34

Reference 36

PREFACE

Mimicry in nature is nothing short of extraordinary. Picture an orchid mantis, camouflaged so seamlessly as a flower that it fools not just its prey, but even the human eye. Or imagine a dead leaf butterfly, its intricate patterns indistinguishable from a dried leaf lying on the forest floor. These marvels of deception are just the beginning. Among the masters of mimicry are longhorn beetles that remarkably resemble wasps

The genus *Necydalis* is known for its wasp mimicry. This group includes approximately 50 species worldwide, about 10 of which are found in Japan. From these, I will introduce five species that can be observed in Japan.

Necydalis beetles are familiar to insect enthusiasts, especially those fond of longhorn beetles, but their remarkable mimicry is intriguing enough to capture the interest of people who may not normally pay attention to insects.

All the photographs in this book were taken in natural environments without any collection. I hope they inspire you to appreciate the joy and wonder of encountering these creatures in the wild.

Necydalis niimurai Hayashi, 1949, stat. rev.
(Jul. 3, 2016, 12:24, Yamanashi. Pref.)

1. WHY MIMIC WASPS?

Mimicry is an extraordinary survival strategy. By mimicking wasps, which many predators instinctively avoid, these beetles reduce their chances of being targeted. This adaptation not only boosts their survival rate but also creates a fascinating illusion for human observers.

Yet, every time I photograph these beetles, I can't help but wonder, "Why is the mimicry so detailed?" Observing them in flight, it's nearly impossible to distinguish whether the insect is a wasp or a longhorn beetle.

While it is clear that the genus *Necydalis* mimics wasps for protection, the precision of their mimicry is astonishing. They even resemble parasitic ichneumon wasps, which adds a fascinating twist: these beetles may imitate the very wasps that parasitize them.

Although it closely resembles an ichneumon wasp, this is actually a longhorn beetle.
Necydalis niimurai Hayashi, 1949, stat. rev. (Jul. 16, 2017, 16:33, Yamanashi Pref.)

Every time I photograph these beetles, I am struck anew by the sheer number of parasitic wasps in their environment. Closer observation reveals that members of the genus *Necydalis* closely mimic these parasitic wasps, adding yet another layer of complexity to their remarkable mimicry.

The irony of a "longhorn beetle mimicking a wasp" being "parasitized by the very wasp it mimics" is both fascinating and difficult to fully articulate.

Interestingly, not only beetles of the genus *Necydalis*, but also those of the genus *Xylotrechus*, are known for their wasp mimicry. In English, these beetles are often referred to as "WASP MIMIC BEETLES." This term is widely used, especially in Europe (including the United Kingdom), as well as in North America and Australia. The name succinctly captures the essence of their mimicry.

Furthermore, beetles of the genus *Xylotrechus* are specifically referred to as "WASP BEETLES," while those of the genus *Necydalis* are described as "WASP-MIMICKING LONGHORN BEETLES." This distinction highlights the differences in their mimicry strategies and appearances.

Its facial features are strikingly similar to those of a wasp.
Necydalis niimurai Hayashi, 1949, stat. rev. (Jul. 7 , 2017, 16:33, Yamanashi Pref.)

4

Wasp-Mimicking Longhorn Beetles of the Genus *Xylotrechus* ("WASP BEETLES")

Xylotrechus zebratus Matsushita, 1938, (Jun. 2016, Yamanashi Pref.)

Xylotrechus villioni (Villard, 1892) (Sep. 2007, Yamanashi Pref.)

Wasp Species Observed During the Photography of *Necydalis* Beetles

A Species of Ichneumon Wasp (Unidentified), Along with Three Other Unidentified Species.
（Jul. 2016, Yamanashi Pref.）

（Jun. 2016, Yamanashi Pref.）

（Jun. 2020, Yamanashi Pref.）

（Jun. 2024, Yamanashi Pref.）

2. Introduction to Five Species of *Necydalis* Beetles

In Japan, there are 10 species of beetles belonging to the genus *Necydalis*. Here, I will introduce the five species that I was able to photograph.

Necydalis gigantea gigantea Kano, 1933. (Jun. 25, 2023, 14:40, Nagano Pref.)

1) *Necydalis niimurai* Hayashi, 1949, stat. rev.

1) Length: 12.5 - 30.0mm

2) Etymology: Named after Taro Niimura, a Japanese lepidopterist. Initially considered a subspecies of *Necydalis formosana Kano, 1933*, it was elevated to species status in 2018. Despite this, many enthusiasts in Japan still affectionately call it "*formosana*." Incidentally, "*formosana*" means "of Taiwan."

3) Host Plants: Species of the genus *Symplocos* (e.g., *Symplocos tanakana*) and other members of the family Symplocaceae.

4) Photography Period: July

Egg-laying on *Symplocos tanakana*.
Necydalis niimurai Hayashi, 1949, stat. rev. (Jul. 19, 2019, 14:54, Yamanashi Pref.)

Among the genus *Necydalis*, this species is relatively easy to observe. In the Kanto region, it is often found at altitudes of 1,300–1,500 meters. Even within Tokyo, it can be observed in locations such as Tomin-no-Mori and Mt. Mitou.

For first-time observers, it might be difficult to recognize as a longhorn beetle. It is often seen on standing dead trees of *Symplocos tanakana*.

Necydalis niimurai Hayashi, 1949, stat. rev. (Jul. 7, 2017, 14:41, Yamanashi Pref.)

Necydalis niimurai Hayashi, 1949, stat. rev. (Jul. 14, 2015, 13:07, Yamanashi Pref.)

After taking the photo, I blew on it and it flew away energetically.
Necydalis niimurai Hayashi, 1949, stat. rev. (Jul. 29, 2017, 10:54, Yamanashi Pref.)

Necydalis niimurai Hayashi, 1949, stat. rev. (Jul. 17, 2017, 10:54, Yamanashi Pref.)

Members of the *Necydalis* genus sometimes remain stationary in unique postures.

Necydalis niimurai Hayashi, 1949, stat. rev.　　(Jul. 8, 2018, 15:20, Yamanashi Pref.)

It is feeding on fungi that have grown on a *Symplocos tanakana*.

Necydalis niimurai Hayashi, 1949, stat. rev.　　(Jul. 29, 2017, 11:14, Yamanashi Pref.)

Larger individuals can often be found near the roots of *Symplocos tanakana*.
Necydalis niimurai Hayashi, 1949, stat. rev.　(Jul 3, 2016, 14:45, Yamanashi Pref.)

Necydalis niimurai Hayashi, 1949, stat. rev. (Jul 3, 2016, 10:54, Yamanashi Pref.)

2) *Necydalis solida* Bates, 1884.

1) Length: 11.4 - 32.0mm
2) Etymology: The origin of the species name "*solida*" remains unknown, although it appears in the scientific names of various plants, shells, and corals.
3) Host Plants: Broadleaf trees, especially beech.
4) Photography Period: Mid-June to Early July

Necydalis solida Bates, 1884. (Jun 28, 2015, 14:15, Yamanashi Pref.)

While it is well known to gather on beech trees, in mixed forests of beech and chestnut, it was often observed on standing dead chestnut trees. In these mixed forests, it was seen from mid-June but was no longer spotted after mid-July.

Necydalis solida Bates, 1884. (Jun 28, 2015, 14:47, Yamanashi Pref.)

Necydalis solida Bates, 1884. (Jul 3, 2016, 12:04, Yamanashi Pref.)

Necydalis solida Bates, 1884. (Jul 3, 2016, 14:55, Yamanashi Pref.)

Necydalis solida Bates, 1884. (Jun 16, 2016, 13:07, Yamanashi Pref.)

A pseudoscorpion, a small arachnid resembling a scorpion but without a tail, clamped onto the middle leg.

Necydalis solida Bates, 1884. (Jun 25, 2020, 12:17, Yamanashi Pref.)

Necydalis solida Bates, 1884. (Jul 10, 2021, 14:32, Yamanashi Pref.)

Necydalis solida Bates, 1884.　(Jul 7, 2017, 12:17, Yamanashi Pref.)

Necydalis solida Bates, 1884. (Jun 14, 2017, 12:45, Yamanashi Pref.)

3) *Necydalis harmandi harmandi* Pic, 1902.

1) Length: 10.5 - 21.8mm

2) Etymology: The name "*harmandi*" was dedicated to Dr. J. Harmand, a French diplomat who contributed to diplomatic relations between Japan and France, particularly around the time of the First Sino-Japanese War and the Russo-Japanese War, from the late 19th to the early 20th century. The name can also be found in the scientific name *Leptura (Strangalia) harmandi* Pic, 1901, which is now considered a subspecies of *Leptura mimica* Bates, 1884. It appears that his name is also found in other insect species, such as *Eumantispa harmandi* and *Isodontia harmandi* (Perez, 1905)."

3) Host Plants: Broadleaf trees.

4) Photography Period: Late July to Early August

Necydalis harmandi harmandi Pic, 1901. (Aug. 4, 2015, 13:34, Gunma Pref.)

Necydalis harmandi harmandi Pic, 1901. (Aug. 24, 2017, 13:34, Yamanashi Pref.)

I photographed this species on the same standing dead chestnut tree where I had previously observed *Necydalis solida* two months earlier. At first glance, I thought it was a wasp, but upon closer inspection, I realized it was a longhorn beetle.

Necydalis harmandi harmandi Pic, 1902. (Jul 31, 2019, 11:19, Yamanashi Pref.)

Necydalis harmandi harmandi Pic, 1901. (Aug. 4, 2015, 13:34, Gunma Pref.)

4) *Necydalis odai* Hayashi, 1951.

1）Length: 11.0 - 25.4 mm

2）Etymology: Named after "Oda," who first collected it in 1948. Enthusiasts often call it *"odai."*

3）Host Plants: Mizunara oak (*Quercus crispula*), the only known host.

4）Photography Period: Late July to Early August

It's easy to overlook if you're not paying close attention.
Necydalis odai Hayashi, 1951. (Jul. 31, 2019, 10:23, Yamanashi Pref.)

Individuals can sometimes be seen on dead parts of mizunara oak trees or flying through forested areas.

It is relatively difficult to find, possibly because it is distributed in mountainous and subalpine regions where mizunara oak is its host plant, and its emergence period in the observed environment is extremely short, lasting only about two weeks.

Necydalis odai Hayashi, 1951. (Jul. 31, 2019, 10:23, Yamanashi Pref.)

A female laying eggs inside a tree cavity
Necydalis odai Hayashi, 1951. (Aug. 9, 2022, 12:32, Yamanashi Pref.)

The following images show the exterior of the cavity and the first sighting of this species.

Inside the Mizunara oak cavity. It's small but keep looking.
Necydalis odai Hayashi, 1951. (Aug. 9, 2022, 12:09, Yamanashi Pref.)

1) Length: 19.8 - 36.0 mm

2) Etymology: The species name "*gigantea*" means "giant" in Latin, reflecting its status as the largest *Necydalis* species.

3) Host plants: A wide range of trees, including mulberry, zelkova, chestnut, and beech.

4) Photography Period: Late June

※　All of the following photographs were taken in Nagano Prefecture on June 25, 2023, around 2:40 PM.

Until I confirmed it with my camera, I was skeptical whether it was a paper wasp or a longhorn beetle.

This species is distributed nationwide and is introduced as Japan's representative "National *Necydalis*" (1).

Old mulberry trees once served as the primary host plants for this species. Historically, mulberry trees were widely cultivated in Japan to support the silk industry. However, as silk production declined, the number of mulberry trees drastically decreased, and by around the year 2000, they had nearly disappeared.

As a result, this species has become increasingly rare. In recent years, it has also been found on old zelkovas and other trees, highlighting its ability to utilize a variety of host plants.

The scientific name *Necydalis* is derived from Greek and is said to have been used by Aristotle to describe "the cocoon of the silkworm that produces silk" (2).

Based on this etymology, one might imagine the origin of *Necydalis* as a "wasp-like longhorn beetle living on mulberry leaves." This connection between mimicry, silk production, and the beetle's history offers a fascinating glimpse into the intersection of natural history and human industry.

3. Videos of Three Species of *Necydalis* Beetles

You can watch videos of the three species of *Necydalis* introduced in this book via the QR code below. These videos were captured during breaks between photo sessions and feature short clips showcasing their behaviors. Some footage may include minor focus issues, and we appreciate your understanding.

Video Content

Necydalis niimurai
(1) Behavior near the base of the tree
(2) Behavior on standing deadwood
(3) Mating and oviposition

Necydalis solida
(1) Mating and oviposition
(2) Behavior on standing deadwood

Necydalis odai
Oviposition inside a hollow

4. Afterword

Thank you for reading this far.

When I first picked up a camera, I was moved by how insects seamlessly blended into their surroundings. However, after years of observing *Necydalis* beetles, I came to see mimicry not merely as a predator-prey interaction but as something that embodies the very essence of the "landscape."

Unfortunately, this "landscape" is becoming harder to witness with each passing year, leaving me with feelings of sadness and frustration. Even so, I hope to continue seeking out the landscapes where insects still remain, however scarce they may be.

Necydalis niimurai Hayashi, 1949, stat. rev.   (Jun 30, 2018, 16:13, Yamanashi Pref.)

When observing insects outdoors, I recommend using tools like a camera or binoculars. As introduced in this book, you can closely examine details such as longhorn beetles that mimic wasps. Additionally, you may notice delicate movements and patterns that are difficult to detect with the naked eye.

Spending time observing and photographing insects, surrounded by natural light, wind, and birdsong, and occasionally in the rain, is an irreplaceable and precious experience. Immerse yourself in the natural landscapes woven by insects, and savor the profound charm they offer through all your senses.

Necydalis solida Bates, 1884. (Jul 18, 2020, 11:32, Yamanashi Pref.)

Office Atact (Insect in the Landscape)
Contact Information
Please use the email form.

Reference

（1） Mushi-sha. (2018) The longhorn beetles of Japan (Iconographic Series of Insect No. 10, pp. 271-284). Tokyo, Japan: Mushi-sha.

（2） Keiichi Kusama: Research history of the genus *Necydalis*. ELYTRA, vol. 1 No. 1-Nov. 1973, vol 2, No.1-May 1974 (The Journal of Japanese Society of Coleopterology).

Office Atact Website

1 Longhorn Beetles in the Landscape

This website features landscape photographs of longhorn beetles. All photos were taken outdoors, and no specimens were collected. Since identification is based solely on the photographs, there may be errors, and the content should not be used for definitive species identification. If you find any errors, we kindly ask for your feedback. We will promptly correct or remove the information. You can access the website via the QR code below.

2 Insects in the Landscape

This website features beetles (*Coleoptera*) and true bugs (*Hemiptera*) other than longhorn beetles. Similar to the landscapes featuring longhorn beetles, identification is based solely on photographs, so the content should not be used for definitive species identification.
If you find any errors, we kindly ask for your feedback. We will promptly correct or remove the information. You can access the website via the QR code below.